Animals in My Yard

Foxes

by Amy McDonald

BELLWETHER MEDIA
MINNEAPOLIS, MN

BLASTOFF!
Beginners

Blastoff! Beginners are developed by literacy experts and educators to meet the needs of early readers. These engaging informational texts support young children as they begin reading about their world. Through simple language and high frequency words paired with crisp, colorful photos, Blastoff! Beginners launch young readers into the universe of independent reading.

Blastoff! Universe

Blastoff! Beginners — Reading Level — Grade K

Blastoff! Readers — Grades 1-3

Blastoff! Discovery — Grade 4

Sight Words in This Book 🔍

a	day	is	the
all	eat	make	their
and	good	may	they
are	have	people	too
at	his	see	under
by	in	some	what

This edition first published in 2021 by Bellwether Media, Inc.

No part of this publication may be reproduced in whole or in part without written permission of the publisher. For information regarding permission, write to Bellwether Media, Inc., Attention: Permissions Department, 6012 Blue Circle Drive, Minnetonka, MN 55343.

Library of Congress Cataloging-in-Publication Data

Names: McDonald, Amy, author.
Title: Foxes / by Amy McDonald.
Description: Minneapolis, MN : Bellwether Media, 2021. | Series: Animals in my yard |
    Includes bibliographical references and index. | Audience: Grades PreK-2
Identifiers: LCCN 2020007339 (print) | LCCN 2020007340 (ebook) | ISBN 9781644873083 (library binding) |
    ISBN 9781681037950 (paperback) | ISBN 9781681037714 (ebook)
Subjects: LCSH: Foxes--Juvenile literature.
Classification: LCC QL737.C22 M3825 2021 (print) | LCC QL737.C22 (ebook) | DDC 599.775--dc23
LC record available at https://lccn.loc.gov/2020007339
LC ebook record available at https://lccn.loc.gov/2020007340

Editor: Christina Leaf   Designer: Jeffrey Kollock

Printed in the United States of America, North Mankato, MN.

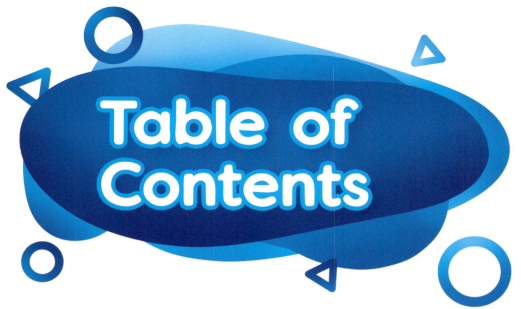

Table of Contents

Foxes!

What is in
the yard?
A fox!

Body Parts

Foxes have thick fur and fluffy tails. They keep warm.

fur

tail

Foxes have
good ears.
They hear food.

ears

Foxes have
sharp teeth.
They bite **prey**.

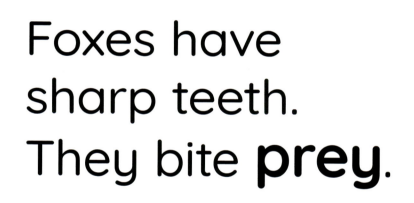

teeth

prey

The Lives of Foxes

Foxes live in **dens**. They are safe in their homes.

den

Foxes may live
by people.
Some make dens
under houses.

Foxes nap
all day in dens.
They hunt
at night.

Foxes eat
rodents.
They eat birds
and berries, too.

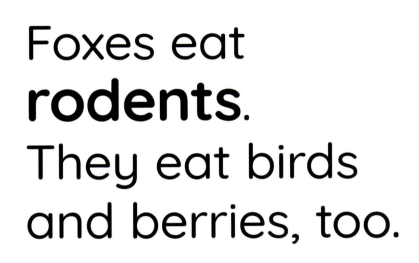

rodents

rodent

birds

berries

19

A father fox brings food home. See his **pups**?

pups

Fox Body Parts

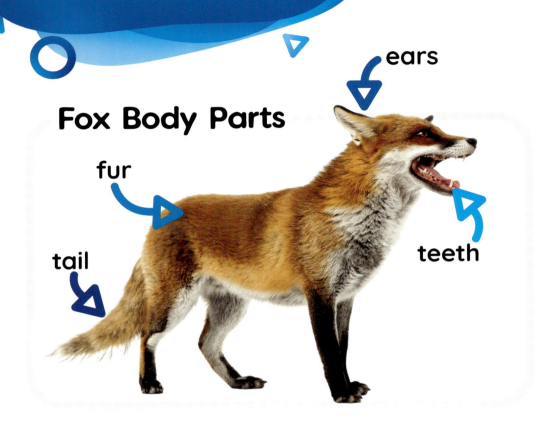

ears

fur

tail

teeth

Fox Food

rodents   birds   berries

Glossary

dens

homes built
by animals

prey

animals that
are hunted

pups

baby foxes

rodents

small, furry
animals

To Learn More

ON THE WEB

FACTSURFER

Factsurfer.com gives you a safe, fun way to find more information.

1. Go to www.factsurfer.com.

2. Enter "foxes" into the search box and click 🔍.

3. Select your book cover to see a list of related content.

Index

The images in this book are reproduced through the courtesy of: olga_gl, front cover; Eric Isselee, pp. 3, 4, 16, 22 (isolated); WildlifeWorld, pp. 4-5; Paul J Hartley, pp. 6-7; Vlada Cech, pp. 8-9; Aquarius Studio, p. 10; scigelova, pp. 10-11; Ed Brown Wildlife/ Alamy, pp. 12-13; Giedriius, pp. 14-15; Dmitry Deshevykh/ Almay, pp. 16-17; Menno Schaefer, pp. 18-19, 22 (birds); Rudmer Zwerver, pp. 18, 23 (rodents); Belen Bilgic Schneider, p. 19 (birds); Igor Normann, p. 19 (berries); Zedenek Machacek, p. 20; Wild Media, pp. 20-21, 23 (pups); Warren Metcalf, p. 22 (rodents); Echunder, p. 22 (berries); Splingis, p. 22 (dens); slowmotiongli, p. 23 (prey).